SURVIVAL TIPS

Richard Spilsbury and Louise Spilsbury

Crabtree Publishing Company
www.crabtreebooks.com

Authors: Richard and Louise Spilsbury
Editor: Kathy Middleton
Production coordinator: Ken Wright
Prepress technician: Margaret Amy Salter
Series consultant: Gill Matthews

Picture Credits:
Corbis: 6, Hulton-Deutsch Collection 28b
Getty Images: Hulton Archive/Zoltan Glass/Stringer 10
Istockphoto: Tamara Murray 25b
Library of Congress: Cover, 20b, 26, Toni Frissell Collection 9, Work Projects Administration Poster Collection 14b
National Archives and Records Administration: Cover, 5, 8, 19b, 21, 27t, 28t
Pat Dean/DHD Multimedia Gallery: Cover
Oregon State Archives: courtesy Northwestern University 23t
Photolibrary Imagestate RM/The National Archives: 22
Shutterstock: Cover, Kuznetsov Alexey 15, Aptyp_kok 14t, Susan Law Cain 29, CreativeHQ 17, Dragon_fang 23b, Ivan Cholakov Gostock-dot-net 4, 7t, Graemo 13, Chris Jenner 11, Neil Roy Johnson 7b, Sergey Kamshylin 24, Joseph McCullar 20t, McIek 27b, Vladimir Melnik 19t, Gina Smith 12t, Charles Taylor 12b, Brian Weed 16t
U.S. Air Force: 16b
Wikimedia Commons: Bibliothèque et Archives nationales du Québec 25t, Andreas Praefcke 18

Library and Archives Canada Cataloguing in Publication

Spilsbury, Richard, 1963-
     WWII survival tips / Richard Spilsbury and Louise Spilsbury.

(Crabtree connections)
Includes index.
ISBN 978-0-7787-9898-9 (bound).--ISBN 978-0-7787-9919-1 (pbk.)

     1. World War, 1939-1945--Evacuation of civilians--Juvenile literature.
2. World War, 1939-1945--Civilian relief--Juvenile literature. 3. Civil defense--Juvenile literature. I. Spilsbury, Louise II. Title.
III. Series: Crabtree connections

D810.C69S64 2011   j940.53   C2010-905301-X

Library of Congress Cataloging-in-Publication Data

Spilsbury, Richard, 1963-
  WWII survival tips / Richard Spilsbury and Louise Spilsbury.
      p. cm. -- (Crabtree connections)
  Includes index.
  ISBN 978-0-7787-9919-1 (pbk. : alk. paper) -- ISBN 978-0-7787-9898-9 (reinforced library binding : alk. paper)
  1. World War, 1939-1945--Evacuation of civilians--Juvenile literature.
2. World War, 1939-1945--Civilian relief--Juvenile literature. 3. Civil defense--Juvenile literature. I. Spilsbury, Louise. II. Title. III. Title: World War II survival tips. IV. Title: World War Two survival tips. V. Series.

    D810.C69S64 2011
    940.53--dc22
                                        2010032440

Printed in the U.S.A./082010/WO20101210

Published in Canada
Crabtree Publishing
616 Welland Ave.
St. Catharines, Ontario
L2M 5V6

Published in the United States
Crabtree Publishing
PMB 59051
350 Fifth Avenue, 59th Floor
New York, New York 10118

Contents

Why You Need this Guide

Everyone should read this guide. It explains some of the important safety skills people need to survive the war.

AIR RAIDS

One of the biggest dangers is **air raids**. These are attacks by planes that drop bombs. Many bombs are dropped near **factories** and cities. Everyone should learn how to recognize warning signals and know what to do and where to go if an air raid happens.

Bombers can travel long distances to drop bombs on foreign towns and cities.

The heavy bombing that is damaging U.K. cities is known as the Blitz.

KEEPING SAFE

Homes and other buildings will be destroyed by the bombs. Bomb blasts cause buildings, glass, brick, and other **debris** to fly everywhere. In fact, most of the injuries in an air raid are caused by flying debris. Following the tips in this guide should help people avoid being injured.

World War II

World War II was fought between 1939 and 1945. On one side were Britain, France, Australia, Canada, New Zealand, India, the Soviet Union, China, and the U.S.A. On the other side were Germany, Italy, and Japan.

Evacuation

In order to keep children safe from bomb attacks, they must be **evacuated.** They will be removed from cities and taken to the countryside. Here, they will stay with other families until it is safe for them to return to their homes.

If children say they do not want to leave, remind them that they are being evacuated for their safety.

WARNING!

Many children will feel scared about leaving their families to go live with strangers and attend new schools. However, it is the duty of every parent to be firm and encourage them to go.

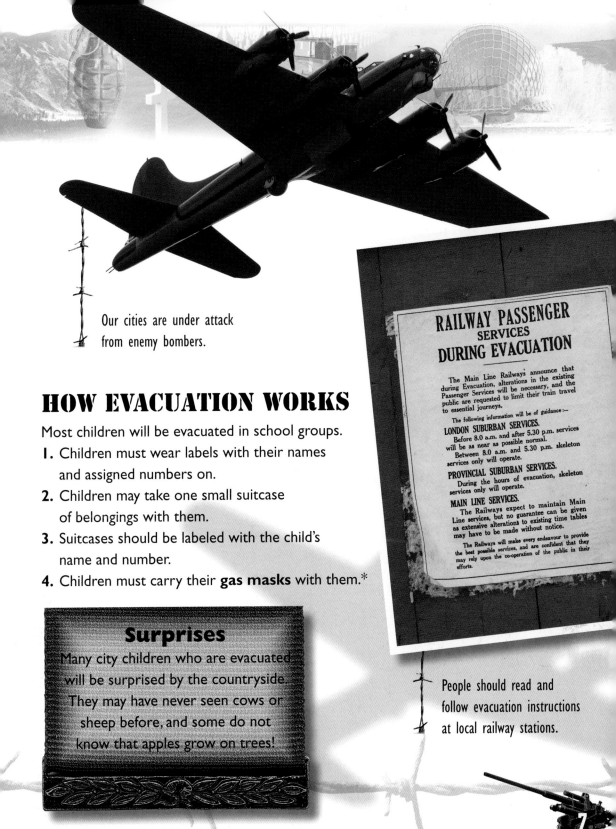

Our cities are under attack
from enemy bombers.

HOW EVACUATION WORKS

Most children will be evacuated in school groups.

1. Children must wear labels with their names
   and assigned numbers on.
2. Children may take one small suitcase
   of belongings with them.
3. Suitcases should be labeled with the child's
   name and number.
4. Children must carry their **gas masks** with them.*

RAILWAY PASSENGER SERVICES DURING EVACUATION

The Main Line Railways announce that during Evacuation, alterations in the existing Passenger Services will be necessary, and the public are requested to limit their train travel to essential journeys.

The following information will be of guidance :—

LONDON SUBURBAN SERVICES.
Before 8.0 a.m. and after 5.30 p.m. services will be as near as possible normal.
Between 8.0 a.m. and 5.30 p.m. skeleton services only will operate.

PROVINCIAL SUBURBAN SERVICES.
During the hours of evacuation, skeleton services only will operate.

MAIN LINE SERVICES.
The Railways expect to maintain Main Line services, but no guarantee can be given as extensive alterations to existing time tables may have to be made without notice.

The Railways will make every endeavour to provide the best possible services, and are confident that they may rely upon the co-operation of the public in their efforts.

Surprises

Many city children who are evacuated will be surprised by the countryside. They may have never seen cows or sheep before, and some do not know that apples grow on trees!

People should read and
follow evacuation instructions
at local railway stations.

* More information about gas masks can be found on pages 16–17 of this book.

Warning Signals

Warning signals are very loud noises
that tell people when they are in danger
from air raids and when it is safe again.
Everyone should learn the different signals.

ALERT AND ALL CLEAR

1. The ALERT signal is a wailing sound.
   It changes from a low to a high note.
   Pay attention! This means enemy planes
   carrying bombs are nearby. The ALERT
   signal is also known as the red warning.
2. The ALL CLEAR signal, or white
   warning, is a note that does not change.
   This means the bomb threat is over.

 WARNING!

People should never stand
by a **siren** without wearing
earplugs, because it is so loud
it could damage their ears!

As soon as a lookout spots an enemy
plane, he will sound the alarm.

WHAT TO DO IN AN AIR RAID

Most air raids happen at night, but do not be caught off guard! Sirens can sound at any time.

1. People should learn where their nearest public air raid shelter is. Some are in tunnels or cellars under buildings. Others are in strong towers.
2. When the ALERT signal sounds, people should stop what they are doing and go quickly to a shelter.
3. People should stay in a shelter until the ALL CLEAR sounds.

Many air raid shelters have beds so that people can sleep there overnight.

Wartime tips
People should not panic! They should listen to the **volunteers** who will lead them to safety.

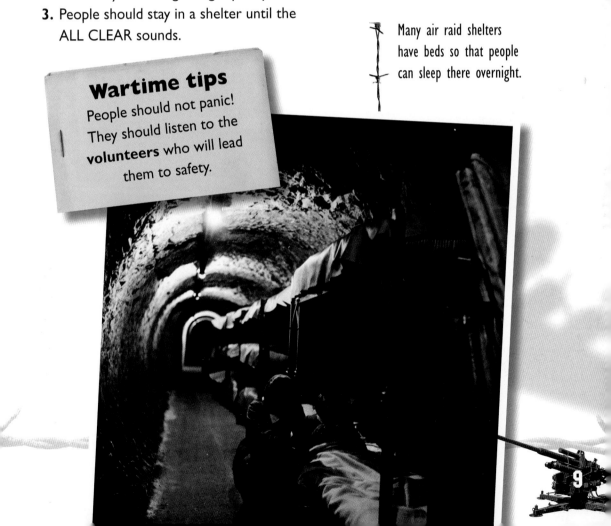

Shelters at Home

Bombs may land on streets and houses. People should build their own air raid shelters at home in case disaster strikes!

WHERE TO SHELTER INSIDE

Here are two suggestions for shelters inside the home:

1. CELLAR: A cellar makes a good shelter, but don't get trapped down there! Debris could block a cellar door, so people should have another way out of the cellar if they need it.

2. CAGE: A Morrison shelter has a metal roof and wire sides. It is a strong, safe cage that goes inside a room. Some people even use it as a table by covering it over with a tablecloth!

Blankets and warm clothing are essential in underground shelters.

Wartime tips
Keep warm! Shelters dug into soil are damp and cold, so people are advised to take coats and blankets inside them.

Camouflage an Anderson shelter by growing grass over it.

MAKE AN OUTDOOR SHELTER

An outdoor shelter in the back yard is the safest option. A simple shelter can be made from a hole in the ground with a wood or metal cover over the top.* A stronger design is called an Anderson shelter. Here is how to make one:

1. Dig a hole in the ground 6.5 feet (2 meters) long, 4.25 feet (1.3 meters) wide, and about 3.25 feet (one meter) deep.
2. Add walls and a curved roof made from sheets of thick steel.
3. Cover the shelter roof with soil to protect against bomb blasts.
4. Put beds and chairs inside.

* Instructions for how to build shelters may be found in newspapers, or people can visit a hardware store for more advice.

Be Prepared

People need to take a box of useful supplies with them into a shelter because air raids can last for many hours. Some people leave the box of supplies in their shelter or have it ready to pick up quickly when a siren sounds.

CHECKLIST FOR THE SUPPLIES BOX

1. food, such as cookies and water
2. candles or gas lamp and matches or lighter
3. blankets and sweaters
4. books and comics
5. toys, such as cars and dolls
6. waterproof fabric, in case the shelter leaks and water gets in

Wartime tips
Use a tin with a tight lid to keep food dry in the shelter.

Keep water, food, and other basic supplies in a shelter.

Toys will stop children from becoming bored during long air raids.

The force of one bomb blast can shatter all the windows in a street.

HOME SAFETY

- A bomb blast can break windows into small pieces of sharp glass. People should cover all windows with pieces of adhesive tape. This will stop the glass from shattering and causing injuries.
- Lock windows and doors before going to the shelter.

★ **WARNING!**

If a bomb hits power cables and gas pipes, there will be no electricity or gas to light buildings. Keep a candle in every room of the home in case this happens.

Blackout

Everyone must follow blackout rules at night. Blackout means no lights are to be used inside homes or on streets, so enemy planes cannot see where to drop bombs.

AT HOME

Absolutely no light is allowed to be seen through windows or doors. Windows must be covered with blackout material* to prevent light from rooms from showing through. Even with blackout curtains, people should use only candles or dim lights inside.

Use blackout material to stop light from escaping through windows.

BLACKOUT means BLACK

ISSUED BY THE OAKLAND DEFENSE

There are no excuses—blackout means black!

People can pass the time listening to the radio during a blackout.

ON THE STREET

People should not go out at night, unless they have to. It is dangerous outside because streetlights will be turned off, and cars will have slotted covers over their headlights to aim light toward the ground. Any trip should be planned carefully. In many places, signposts have been removed so that, if the enemy **invades**, they will not be able to find their way around.

⊛ WARNING!

People are warned to take care during blackouts. It is easy to get lost or injured by bumping into people, lampposts, and other things. Several people have drowned after falling into rivers or ponds in the dark.

* Blackout material is a thick, black cotton cloth, which you can buy in stores.

Gas Hazards

Enemy planes may drop bombs that release **poisonous** gas into the air. If people breathe this in, they may become ill or die. For protection, everyone will be given a gas mask.

GAS MASKS

- Everyone must carry their gas mask with them at all times.
- There will be **drills** to instruct people on how to use gas masks.
- Gas masks are made of smelly black rubber, so some people may feel sick wearing them.
- The gas mask may mist up when people breathe into it.

If gas bombs are dropped, they can harm or kill people in minutes.

GAS MASK DRILL

Children will practice using their gas masks at school at least once a week by performing the following drill:

1. A teacher will enter the classroom and shout, "Gas!"
2. Children will remove their masks from their boxes quickly.*
3. The mask should be put on the face first and then the straps pulled over the head.
4. The teacher will check that the mask fits correctly.
5. The teacher will remind children to breathe normally when wearing a gas mask.

⭐ WARNING!

People will be forced to pay a fine if they are caught without their gas masks!

This is an adult gas mask. There are special masks for children and babies.

* Mickey Mouse gas masks are available for children to encourage them to wear the mask.

Be Careful

It is vital that people are aware of the dangers that continue after an air raid is over.

BOMB DAMAGE

- People should not touch bombs that have not blown up yet. Butterfly bombs do not **explode** when they hit the ground, but they do go off if people touch them later.
- People should not enter buildings that have been damaged by bombs. The floors or ceilings may fall down while people are walking inside them.

Sharp pieces of **shrapnel** like this can cause serious wounds.

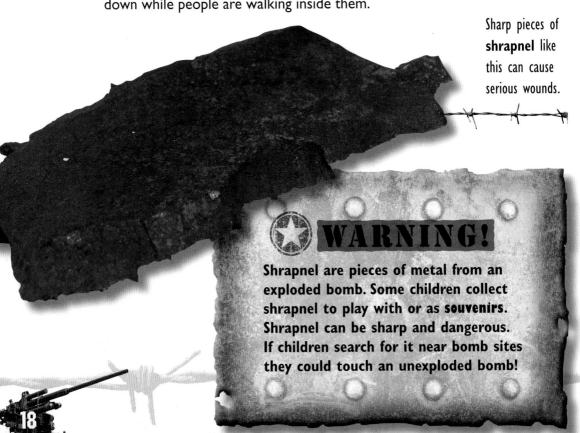

⭐ WARNING!

Shrapnel are pieces of metal from an exploded bomb. Some children collect shrapnel to play with or as **souvenirs**. Shrapnel can be sharp and dangerous. If children search for it near bomb sites they could touch an unexploded bomb!

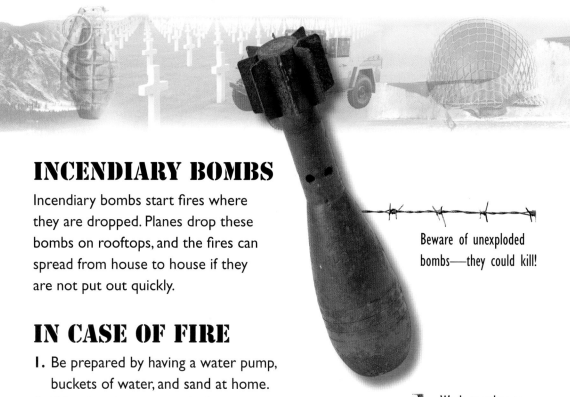

INCENDIARY BOMBS

Incendiary bombs start fires where they are dropped. Planes drop these bombs on rooftops, and the fires can spread from house to house if they are not put out quickly.

Beware of unexploded bombs—they could kill!

IN CASE OF FIRE

1. Be prepared by having a water pump, buckets of water, and sand at home.
2. If fire breaks out, people from a street should work together in teams.
3. Buckets of water and sand should be passed from person to person and thrown on the fire.
4. Teams should work in this way until fire engines arrive.

Work together to control fires until firefighters arrive.

Food Rations

Before the war, many types of food, such as sugar and tea, were **imported**. They were brought in from other countries by ship. These ships are now under attack, so there is less food available. **Rationing** is being introduced so that everyone has a fair share of food.

RATION BOOKS

Everyone will be given their own ration book with coupons or stamps in it. These pieces of printed paper or card show a shopkeeper how much food a person is allowed. People have to use the coupons or stamps when they buy foods, such as meat, butter, and sugar, each week.

41 COFFEE

730301H

4 UNITED STATES OF AMERICA
OFFICE OF PRICE ADMINISTRATION

WAR RATION BOOK FOUR

(Print first, middle, and last names)

50 SPARE

Issued to

Complete address

READ BEFORE SIGNING

In accepting this book, I recognize that it remains the property of the United States Government. I will use it only in the manner and for the purposes authorized by the Office of Price Administration.

(Signature)

Void if Altered   It is a criminal offense to violate rationing regulations.

LS–36510-A

OPA Form R-145

Look after your ration book and do not lose it!

"We are saving you YOU save FOOD"

Well fed Soldiers
WILL WIN the WAR

Remember, by saving food you are helping the war effort.

HOW TO USE RATION BOOKS

1. People should check that a shop has the item of food they want and what its value is in coupons.
2. They should then hand the ration book to the shopkeeper.
3. The shopkeeper will cross off or cut out one of the coupons or stamps.
4. People must then pay the shopkeeper for the food.

Shopkeepers must remove ration coupons or stamps before they give you the food.

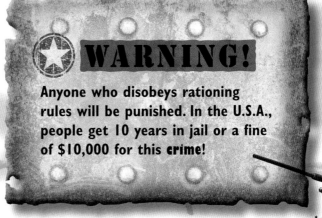

WARNING!

Anyone who disobeys rationing rules will be punished. In the U.S.A., people get 10 years in jail or a fine of $10,000 for this crime!

Dig for Victory

To make sure everyone has enough food to survive the war, people are urged to grow their own. People should dig up their lawns and flower beds, unused ground and parks, and plant fruit and vegetables there instead.*

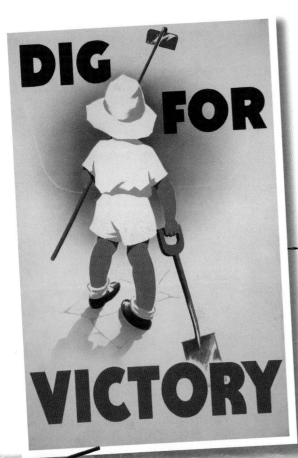

KEEPING ANIMALS

People are also advised to keep their own animals for meat. Chickens can be kept in a small amount of space and will give a family eggs and meat. People could also keep rabbits and goats. Pigs are cheap to feed because they will eat vegetable peelings and leftovers.

Children can help dig and grow vegetables, too!

Home grown

By 1945, 20 million gardens produced almost 40 percent of the vegetables grown in the U.S.A.

STORING FOOD

People should **preserve** food grown in summer, so that it stays fresh to use in winter. Onions can be stored in jars of vinegar, fruit can be stored in jars of sugar and water, and vegetables can be stored in salt water. If **chutneys** are made from vegetables, these can also be used to liven up boring meals.

CARROT TREATS

To make a treat, use home-grown vegetables instead of other foods. Carrots can be used to make:

- Carrolade—a sweet drink made from grated carrots;
- carrot marmalade;
- toffee carrots;
- carrot fudge.

Canning vegetables in jars gives people a year-round supply of food.

PLANT A VICTORY GARDEN

OUR FOOD IS FIGHTING

A GARDEN WILL MAKE YOUR RATIONS GO FURTHER

By growing your own food, you will help to win the war.

* Leaflets will be available explaining what to grow and how to grow it.

Make Do and Repair

It is vital that people do not waste anything during wartime. Many things are in short supply, so people should repair things that break rather than buy new ones.

CLOTHES

Fabric is needed for things like soldiers' uniforms and hospital bedding. Therefore ration books will be provided for people to buy new clothes. People should reuse fabric whenever they can. For example:

- make a dress from old curtains
- turn old pillowcases into shorts or blouses
- use blankets to make coats

Share your bathwater!

To save water, people must only use 5 inches (12.5 cm) of bathwater once a week. In many homes, this may mean families have to take baths in turns and use the same bathwater!

Save material at home so it can be made into uniforms for soldiers.

Collect old rubber tires—they can be recycled into new ones.

LEARN TO KNIT

Civilians are also encouraged to knit to help the country win the war! If people unravel wool from old sweaters, they can knit things for themselves or make socks, sweaters, and scarves for soldiers. For people who do not know how to knit, classes and information leaflets are available.

Children will be given extra clothing coupons to allow for them growing out of clothes.

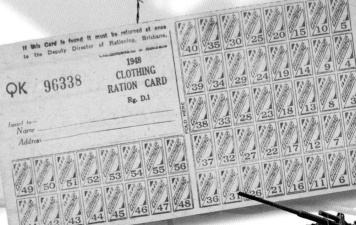

Keeping Cheerful

These are difficult times but it is important for everyone to keep cheerful. People should still go to work and carry out their duties, but also make time to enjoy themselves.

WIRELESS AND MOVIE THEATER

People are advised to remain informed about what is happening in the war by listening to their wireless* every day. People can also listen to their wireless to hear funny shows that keep the family happy. Bus fares and theater tickets will be kept cheap so that everyone can go to the theater to watch films and news reports about the war.

It is suggested that people organize dances, concerts, and shows in their local area for everyone to enjoy.

* The wireless is known to some people as a radio.

AT HOME

There will be no new books for sale, so people should share books with friends or read library books. Writing letters is another way to pass the time. It is good to send news that loved ones away from home are safe and well—especially if they have been evacuated or are fighting in the war.

Even when things are bad, support your friends to keep each other cheerful.

Help children to make their own toys to play with.

Toys

Factories that made children's toys before the war are now making weapons instead. People will have to buy second-hand toys. Children should make their own games from whatever they can find, such as unwanted pieces of wood, paper, or fabric.

In Case of Emergency

If people follow the advice in this book, they should keep safe. However, these are the steps to follow in case something does go wrong.

IF A HOME IS BOMBED

People should not panic. If a street is bombed, rescue teams will arrive to help people out of fallen buildings. Ambulances will take injured people to hospital. Families should already have made plans about where to stay if their house is bombed. In an emergency, most people will be offered food and beds, and loaned clothes or furniture by friends and neighbors.

Call for firefighters immediately to help prevent fires from spreading.

VOLUNTEERS

To be effective in times of emergency, each area needs a group of well-trained volunteers. These are people who give their time to help others. Volunteers may:

- carry messages when telephone services fail;
- show people to safety after an air raid;
- serve drinks and warm food to people who have lost their homes;
- help people to find relatives lost during an air raid.

To survive, everyone should do their duty and help others wherever and whenever they can.

Volunteers use their knowledge of local areas to reunite families.

Glossary

air raids Groups of planes dropping many bombs on one place

chutneys Thick sauces made from vegetables, sugar, vinegar, and spices

civilians People who are not in the air force, army, navy, or police force

crime Action that breaks the law

debris Pieces of wood, metal, glass, and other materials that are left when something is destroyed or broken up

drills Exercises to practice what to do in an emergency

evacuated To be moved from a dangerous place to somewhere safer

explode To blow up with a loud bang

factories Large buildings where things are made, such as shoe factories

fine Money paid for breaking a rule or law

gas masks Devices people wear over their faces to stop them from breathing in dangerous gas

imported When something, such as food, is brought from one country to be sold in another

invades When one country attacks and takes control of another country

poisonous Substance that makes people sick or kills them

preserve To do something to food to keep it fresh and good to eat for a long time

rationing To allow people only a fixed amount of food, so that everyone gets a fair share of what is available

shrapnel Broken pieces of an exploded bomb

siren Machine that makes a loud sound to warn people of danger

souvenirs Objects that someone keeps to help them remember an important event

volunteers People who do jobs without being paid for doing it

Further Information

WEB SITES

Find out more about World War II at:
www.bbc.co.uk/schools/primaryhistory/world_war2

Visit the National World War II Museum in New Orleans at:
www.nationalww2museum.org

See photographs of the home front in the United States from World War II at:
www.archives.gov/research/ww2/photos/#home

Visit the Canadian War Museum at:
www.warmuseum.ca/swm/home/home

Read about the War at Home on this Web site from Virtual Museum Canada at:
www.virtualmuseum.ca/Exhibitions/Militaris/eng/home/home_i1.html

BOOKS

Eyewitness Books: World War II. Dorling Kindersley (2007).

My Secret War Diary, by Flossie Albright: My History of the Second World War 1939–1945 by Marcia Williams. Candlewick Press (2008).

Woeful Second World War (Horrible Histories) by Terry Deary and Martin Brown. Scholastic, re-issue (2007).

World War II for Kids by Richard Panchyk. Chicago Review Press (2002).

Index